Lamar Alexander's
LITTLE
PLAID BOOK

311 rules, reminders, and lessons about running
for office and making a difference,
whether it's for president of the United States or
president of your senior class

RUTLEDGE HII

Nashville, Tenn

Published in Nashville, Tennessee, by Rutledge Hill Press®, 211 Seventh Avenue North, Nashville, Tennessee 37219.

Distributed in Canada by H. B. Fenn & Company, Ltd., 34 Nixon Road, Bolton, Ontario L7E 1W2.

Distributed in Australia by The Five Mile Press Pty., Ltd., 22 Summit Road, Noble Park, Victoria 3174.

Distributed in New Zealand by Tandem Press, 2 Rugby Road, Birkenhead, Auckland 10.

Distributed in the United Kingdom by Verulam Publishing, Ltd., 152a Park Street Lane, Park Stree, St. Albans, Hertfordshire AL2 2AU.

Typography by Compass Communications, Inc., Nashville, Tennessee

Back-cover photo by Robin Hood

ISBN: 1-55853-579-9

Library of Congress Cataloging-in-Publication data available

Printed in the United States of America

1 2 3 4 5 6 7 8 9 — 02 01 00 99 98

INTRODUCTION

Not long ago a young man came by my office. He told me that his dream is to serve in public office. He wanted my advice on how to go about it and what to look out for. I encouraged him and mentioned a few lessons I had learned along the way.

That night, after I had returned home, I decided to finish this book—a project I'd had in mind for a long time—as a gift for that young man as well as for anyone else who has ever thought about running for and serving in office, or is thinking about helping somebody else do it.

Whether your dream is to serve as president of your senior class or president of the United States, or to volunteer

in a campaign, my hope is that this *Little Plaid Book* will
encourage you to experience for yourself the excitement
of campaigning and the satisfaction of making a difference.

—LAMAR ALEXANDER
Nashville, Tennessee
April 1998

- You may be thinking that this book looks a lot like *Life's Little Instruction Book* or one of those other little books that H. Jackson Brown, Jr. writes. Don't worry. Jack's a friend of mine, and I asked him about it. He not only said it's OK, but he helped me. And we had a good time doing it.

- Most of these rules, lessons, and reminders are my own. Some I've borrowed, giving credit when I've known the source.

- **All my profits from this *Little Plaid Book,* after taxes, will go to scholarships for Maryville (Tenn.) High School graduates and to other charitable activities.**

CONTENTS

THE STORY OF THE
RED AND BLACK PLAID SHIRT

In 1978, during my campaign for governor, I walked for six months and one thousand miles across Tennessee. I wore a red and black plaid shirt every day. Some people made fun of it, but when one sweaty shirt brought five hundred dollars at an auction, I knew my stock was going up. The shirt became the trademark of a winning grassroots campaign. Now, wherever I go in Tennessee, someone will smile and ask, "Where's the shirt?"

In 1995 I announced my candidacy for president and took a walk through Maryville, my hometown. Again I wore my red and black plaid shirt. The national news media had a conniption fit. The late *Chicago Tribune* columnist Mike Royko wrote, "Not fit for a possum!" But my supporters began showing up everywhere in plaid shirts, plaid skirts, plaid ties, plaid socks, and even plaid shorts. Margaret Hough, Iowa governor Terry Branstad's assistant, made a beautiful red and black plaid dress and wore it to work. Governor Branstad was then serving as Sen. Bob Dole's campaign chairman. Fortunately for Margaret, the governor had as good a sense of humor as she did.

In March 1996, a few days after I withdrew from the presidential race, Bob Dole came to Maryville, the national media in tow. To symbolize my support, I presented him with one of my shirts—prompting Sen. Howard Baker to take the stage and say, "I hope that's his last one!"

Well, it wasn't. I have plenty left. They still fit and I still wear them. The plaid brigade of supporters still seems to be wearing them, too—and I'm awfully glad they are. At the 1997 Lincoln Day dinner in Belknap County, New Hampshire, Jim Hughes, the winner of the door prize, was neatly dressed in a coat, tie—and red and black plaid shirt.

Looking back at the presidential race, I'm afraid that too many people remembered my shirt better than they did my message, which was that we must learn to expect less from government and more of ourselves. But the red and black plaid carried—and still carries—its own message. It became the symbol of a grassroots campaign in which people could get involved, have a good time, and actually make a difference.

Lamar Alexander's

LITTLE

PLAID BOOK

I

CAMPAIGNING AND SURVIVING CHEERFULLY

Take your office seriously, but don't take yourself too seriously.

1. Wear your red and black plaid shirt, but not when you announce for president of the United States.

2. Know the price of milk, bread, and eggs. I couldn't remember them one day during the 1996 New Hampshire primary, and the media had a good time at my expense.

3. Know from the first day of your campaign what you will do your first day in office.

4. Be yourself, speak from the heart, and not for too long.

5. If you want a standing ovation, seat a few friends in the front row.

6. Don't step on your applause lines.

7. If you don't have any applause lines, borrow some.

8. **Never speak on a subject about which the audience knows more than you do.**

—Lady Margaret Thatcher

9. Tell stories, but keep them short. David's encounter with Goliath is told in 327 words.

10. If you are introduced to speak after 10:00 P.M., tell one story, offer one inspirational thought, thank your audience, and sit down.

11. If after your speech the master of ceremonies says, "And now if anyone is still awake, we have time for questions," take no questions. I am embarrassed to admit this actually happened to me late one evening in a little town in Colorado.

12. Consider yourself in trouble if you say, "And now in conclusion," and the audience starts to applaud.

13. If you want to give a really fired-up speech, you might want to try this: Sit in your car with the windows rolled up, turn the gospel music radio station up as loud as it will go, listen for fifteen minutes, then jump right out and start speaking. The rhythm of the music will become the rhythm of your speech.

> *—According to his sister, Sen. Anna Belle Clement O'Brien, this is one way former Tennessee governor Frank Clement got ready to make a speech.*

14. Tell the truth. It's the right thing to do, and it will confuse your opponent.

15. Use words judiciously.

> **Don't just choose your words for what they mean. Choose them for how they taste.**
>
> —*Sen. Everett McKinley Dirksen*

16. Treat every microphone and every TV camera as "on."

17. If you don't know the answer, say, "I don't know."

18. Remember that "Yes" and "No" are also perfectly acceptable answers.

19. Give concise answers. The Center for Media Affairs reports that the average sound bite of presidential candidates on network news during the 1996 campaign was seven seconds.

20. If you answer some question other than the one you were asked just because you read somewhere that this is the clever thing to do, remember that people watching on TV will think of you as clever instead of honest.

21. Start your campaign and hang on until the finish. In more cases than you might imagine, this is all that it takes to win.

22. Remember that you can't win the race at the start—but you sure can lose it there.

23. **Be careful where you aim. You're likely to get there.**

—*Chet Atkins, guitarist*

24. Aim for the top. There's more room there.

—*R. R. Rankin, my grandfather*

25. Be on time.

26. Be specific. People are looking for answers.

27. Be optimistic. Most American movies have happy endings.

28. If you grew up in a small town, be grateful. There is something about it that encourages achievement and adventure.

29. Don't forget that knowing where you are can be just as important as what you have to say.

In Pella, Iowa, I once shook hands with everyone seated for dinner and got halfway through the food line before someone asked, "Are you sure you're in the right place?" and I realized I had walked into a truckers' Christmas party instead of the Republican meeting that was in the room across the hall.

30. Answer these questions one hundred times in front of a mirror: "Why am I running?" and "What do I hope to accomplish?"

31. Repeat your answers again and again in your speeches and in your interviews until your family and friends are sick of listening—for that's when it's just beginning to sink in with everybody else.

32. The bottom line is this: If you don't have a better reason to run for office than William J. Bular did, find something else to do. While campaigning for governor of South Dakota in 1932, he declared, "There are no issues. My opponent has a job, and I want it. That's what this election is all about."

33. Know when to stand up.
    Know when to speak up.
    Know when to shut up.

    —*Benjamin Disraeli*

34. Think twice before speaking for more than twenty minutes. Neither the bottom nor the brain can absorb much more.

35. Try not to let your tongue run faster than your brain.

36. Be aware that what you are saying may not be what people are hearing you say.

37. Sound like yourself, not like some broadcaster.

When you stop sounding like where you grew up is when you start getting into trouble.

—*Roy Blount Jr.*

38. Shake hands until you have to put Band-Aids on your blisters. People still want to touch their politicians when they hear their politics.

39. If you want to avoid colds, wash your hands after shaking lots of hands. Ronald Reagan once told me that this was his doctor's advice.

40. If you want to get something done, give someone else the credit.

41. Remember names as if the election depends on it. It does.

42. To help in remembering names, try to remember one thing special about each person you meet.

43. And when you are meeting someone, don't be looking at someone else.

44. Seize the opportunity before it ceases to be an opportunity.

> **I seen my opportunities and I took 'em.**
>
> —*George Washington Plunkitt, Tammany Hall boss*

45. Spend time with voters and not too much time with political big shots. Big shots can defeat you, but they can't elect you.

46. Treat every friendly reporter as a reporter doing his or her job.

47. Treat every unfriendly reporter as a reporter doing his or her job.

48. Don't expect the media to understand your position if you don't tell them.

49. Don't be surprised when the media don't understand your position, even if you do tell them.

50. Treat every interview as "on the record." Then you won't have to remember what was off the record.

51. Don't try to write the reporter's story, even if you're sure you can write it better yourself.

52. Never let a charge go unanswered.

53. When answering a charge, don't repeat the charge.

54. **If you sling a pail of mud, expect a load of garbage back in the face.**

—*Hubert H. Humphrey*

55. Watch your step.

Politics is more dangerous than war, for in war you are only killed once.

—*Winston S. Churchill*

56. Don't do anything today that you don't want to read about tomorrow.

57. Be surprised only if there are no surprises.

58. If something embarrassing happens, announce it yourself before someone else does.

59. If it was a mistake and you did it, admit it, and don't do it again.

60. Avoid these phrases when describing what went wrong:

"Mistakes were made."
"I am not a crook."
"No controlling legal authority."

61. Keep in mind the basics.

> **I'll tell you how to get elected. First, don't make any promises— we've heard them all before. Just do the best you can. Second, keep the taxes down; we can't afford more. Third, for heaven's sakes, behave yourself when you get in! We're sick and tired of being embarrassed by all those politicians we hear about on the radio.**

> *—Hawkins County woman on my walk across Tennessee*

62. When in doubt, don't.

63. If it looks suspicious, assume it is.

64. If someone can't explain it, don't believe it.

65. Keep in mind that there are only two ways to run for office: scared and unopposed.

—*Texas proverb as reported by Jim Lehrer*

66. Remember that it's never too early to raise money.

> **Early money helps the most, is appreciated the best, and remembered the longest.**
>
> —*Ted Welch, America's No. 1 Republican fundraiser*

67. When raising money, don't forget to ask for the money.

68. Never confuse pledges with money in the bank.

69. Never take cash.

70. Hire a good accountant.

71. Hold at least one $100-a-plate fundraising dinner, where, for $200, the donor can stay home.

72. Studies show that one-half a campaign's money is wasted. Hire a campaign manager who can figure out which half.

73. Walk in parades.

74. If it is the Mule Day parade, walk at the front.

75. Be well organized, but be surprised if your campaign is.

76. Never organize a campaign so well that it can't burst out of control to win.

77. **Never wear a hat that has more character than you do.**

—*Lance Morrow*

78. Before playing a harmonica in public, think about how it will look on TV. That's why, following my wife's advice, I play the piano and keep my harmonica in my pocket.

79. Don't ignore local radio. Voters trust it.

80. Don't ignore newspapers. They set the political agenda in a way TV never can.

81. Never ignore TV. It introduces you to the voters in a way newspapers never can.

82. Never pass up an opportunity to appear on C-Span. C-Span viewers vote.

83. Buy TV ads early.
Buy TV ads late.
Buy as many TV ads as you can.

84. Don't shout when on TV. The camera may be several feet away, but the microphone is usually right under your nose and microphones aren't hard of hearing.

85. Never fake anything. The camera shows what is real.

86. Imagine that the camera is your best friend.

When on TV, say with your eyes to the camera, "I'm glad to be here. I'm glad you're here. I'm looking forward to talking with you."

—*Merrie Spaeth*

87. Remember that the Internet and twenty-four-hour TV news channels create new opportunities to get out good news—and to spread bad news like wildfire.

88. If you want media coverage, pick a fight.

89. If you want serious media coverage, pick a fight in Washington, D.C.

90. If you are on the radio, don't be surprised if people come up and want to talk with you.

91. If you are on TV, don't be surprised if people come up and just stare at you—and then say strange things.

For example, after staring at me for a long while, one man asked, "Ain't you Alexander?"

"Yes, sir," I said.

"You shore don't favor yourself," he said.

92. Try to get enough rest.

93. Pack extra dress shirts or blouses.

94. Eat a hearty breakfast. It might be your only good meal that day.

95. When you're really stuck for an answer, ask your mother or grandmother for advice.

96. If you don't have time to hear a story about someone else's grandchild, you're probably not the kind of person who ought to serve in public office.

97. If you're running for president, be prepared to answer this question: "Sir, I'm ready to fight and die for my country. How have you prepared yourself to give that order?" I'll never forget the night a nineteen-year-old airman asked it of me.

98. Plan your work and work your plan.

99. **Never interfere with your opponent's self-destruction.**

—Lee Atwater

100. Never have more chairs than people at a political event.

101. Never hold a political event in a room large enough to hold everyone who shows up.

102. **Beware of advisers who are always hearing things that are never said.**

—Harry S Truman

103. Help your spouse find a campaign mission, too.

The wives of politicians deserve a trust fund for their part in campaigning, not to mention the five-minute speeches they are called upon to give when they represent their husbands, plus a bonus for every speech they've heard eighty-five times and remained awake.

—*Erma Bombeck*

104. Win. There's no prize for second.

105. If you want to win, set the agenda.

106. Don't ever complain about being the front-runner.

107. Hold something in reserve.

108. Never give up.

109. Never waste time listening to a politician tell you how he or she won an election. They rarely have a clue.

110. Don't be surprised if winning isn't all you thought it might be. Winning can be a lot like turning thirteen: Much of the joy of the moment will have been used up in anticipation of the event.

111. On election night be prepared for bad news to arrive as hard and fast as the sound of a gunshot.

112. Keep a graceful concession speech handy.

113. Know that being the losing candidate at your own victory party will be the closest you'll ever come to experiencing your own funeral.

114. If you lose, don't be afraid to try again.

From a lot of at-bats eventually come some hits.

—Tom Peters

115. But don't be a threat to every vacancy.

Whenever I see a throne, I have the urge to sit on it.

—Napoleon Bonaparte

116. When you lose, the best thing to do is to go to bed as early as possible.

117. When you win, remember the turtle on top of the fence post. Both of you will have had some help getting there.

II
Learning along the Way

There is no school for practical politics.
Most people learn by jumping in feet first.

118. Before running for any office, take a vow of humility.

You'll spend most of your time hoping what happened to Congressman Mo Udall doesn't happen to you. He walked into a barbershop in New Hampshire and said, "I'm Mo Udall, running for president."

"Yeah, I know," the barber said. "We were just laughing about that yesterday."

119. Don't expect everybody to be just standing there anxious to shake your hand.

While walking across New Hampshire, I met a woman who was taking a smoke break from her work at a shoe factory. I stuck out my hand and said, "I'm Lamar Alexander. I'd like to be your next president." She looked at me and at my red and black plaid shirt, blew a little smoke in my face, and said with some disgust, "That's all we need—another president!"

120. Don't expect even your strongest supporters always to agree with your campaign strategy.

Early in my campaign for the presidency, I telephoned Sen. Howard Baker. "I've decided to walk across New Hampshire, from Concord to the sea," I told him.

Senator Baker said, "If I were doing it, I'd walk from Portsmouth to the sea."

"Portsmouth is on the sea," I said.

"I know," he said.

121. Listen to your spouse.

122. This is important, so I'll say it again: Listen to your spouse.

> **When I was younger, my wife would say as I rose to speak, "Say something worthwhile." As I grew older, she said, "Keep it short." Now she says, "Hold in your stomach."**
>
> *—Lee Dreyfus, former Wisconsin governor*

123. If you want to be noticed, don't ride in a convertible with Dolly Parton.

At the opening day of the Dollywood theme park in 1986, I rode through the crowd with Dolly in a 1909 Lewis Roadster. Several people shouted, "Governor, would you please move over so we can see Dolly?"

124. Be especially careful when you stay up late and get up early.

After a long day of campaigning, I arrived in Marietta, Georgia, well after midnight. The local committee insisted that I spend the night at a bed-and-breakfast. The owner insisted that

I get up early the next morning to try her "special muffins."

So, about 6:00 A.M., I stumbled downstairs. There was the lady, the kitchen table, the "special muffins," a pitcher of orange juice, the coffee, and a coffee cup. I proceeded to do something I've never done before and am not likely to do again. I picked up the orange juice and poured it into the coffee cup.

The lady looked at me for a long time and finally said, "I sure hope you're not running for anything big."

125. Don't pay too much for an out-of-town speaker.

In Scott County, Tennessee, the meeting of the Republican Executive Committee turned to the question of who should speak at the Lincoln Day dinner. One wanted Goldwater. One said Rockefeller. One wanted Reagan. Another said Nixon. Finally, someone asked the chairman of the committee, "Homer, what do you think? Who should be our speaker?"

"Well," the chairman replied, "to tell the truth, when I'm up and a-goin' good, I reckon I'd just as soon hear me as anybody."

126. Be prepared to accept rejection.

During the first hour of the first day of my thousand-mile walk across Tennessee, I walked up to a man who was sitting inside a pickup truck. This was at the Broadway Food Market, two blocks from the house where I had grown up. The man's truck window was rolled down, so I stuck out my hand and said, "I'm Lamar Alexander and I'd like to be your next governor." The truck driver quickly rolled up his window and drove away.

127. Never tamper with success.

The legendary football coach Bear Bryant of Alabama had recruited the nation's best punter. During practice, Coach Bryant stood silently and watched intently as the young man boomed punt after punt seventy yards or more. Day after day, the coach never said a word. Finally, the punter, exasperated, said, "Coach, I came all the way to Alabama to play for the best coach in America and you've never said a word to me about my kicking!"

"Son," Bear Bryant said, "when you kick it fifty yards, I'll remind you what you were doing when you were kicking it seventy yards."

128. Don't spend too much time on macroeconomics.

Walking through Pembroke, New Hampshire, I stopped at Lang's Ice Cream Shop and ordered a chocolate ice cream cone, which must have been a foot high. "I'd like to pay for the ice cream," I told the owner, whose name was Virginia Jennings.

"Of course not," Virginia said.

"But I'd like to help the economy," I said.

"Don't worry about it," she said. "I *am* the economy."

129. If you set out to fix the schools, expect a fight.

School reform is the hardest, meanest, bloodiest thing I've ever tried to do.

—Ross Perot told me this in 1984

130. Don't get all puffed up just because you've been on TV.

Television can make a star out of a mule. The biggest crowd we ever had at Hillbilly Homecoming in my hometown of Maryville was in 1955. That's when "Francis the Talking Mule," a mule with its own TV show, was flown in just to walk in our parade. We had mules all over our county, but the largest crowd in history turned out for that parade for one reason: They wanted to see Francis *because that mule had been on TV.*

131. Unless you want to know, don't ask.

After one of my speeches, I overheard someone say, "Worst speech I ever heard."

"Who is that?" I asked the county chairman.

"Oh, the town nitwit," said the chairman. "All he does is go around and repeat what everybody else is saying."

132. Again, if you don't want to know, don't ask.

As he was being introduced in Nashville, President Bush turned to Barbara Bush and asked, "What should I speak about?"

"About five minutes, George," Barbara said.

133. Stop griping and run for office yourself.

Will Rogers had listened to his fellow Oklahomans describe their congressman as a liar, philanderer, and thief. There was nothing bad about him they didn't say. Finally, one of the complainers said, "Will, you're from here. What do you think?"

"Well," Will Rogers said, "I know the congressman. I know the district. My opinion is that the congressman is pretty well representative of most of the people in the district."

134. Remember that sometimes it's best to smile and say nothing.

One Saturday morning in Dover, New Hampshire, I was sitting on the curb having a bagel for breakfast. A man recognized me.

"You're Lamar Alexander, aren't you?"

"Yes, I am."

He looked again.

"No, you're not," he said and walked away.

135. And never forget what is really important.

When I was appointed education secretary, one newspaper wrote, "Mr. Alexander grew up in a lower-middle-class family in the mountains of Tennessee." That was all right with me, but I found out when I called home the next week, it was not all right with my mother. She was literally reading Thessalonians to gather strength for how to deal with this slur on the family.

"We never thought of ourselves that way," she said. "You had a library card from the day you were three and music lessons from the day you were four. You had everything you needed that was important."

136. Be grateful for any compliment.

On my first day as president of the University of Tennessee, a faculty member said, "Mr. Alexander, I so much enjoyed hearing Dick Estell read your book about Australia on National Public Radio."

"Thank you very much," I said.

The faculty member began to walk away, but then she turned around and said to me, "Oh, I just love Dick Estell. I believe he could make the telephone book sound interesting!"

137. When elected, be prepared to serve.

Late one night at the governor's mansion, I received a call from a constituent who asked me to come pick up his garbage. "Why, of course," I said, "I'll be glad to come get your garbage. But tell me, why did you call the governor to come pick up your garbage? Why didn't you call the garbage man?"

"Because I didn't want to go that high," came the reply.

138. Expect the truth from children.

At a fundraiser in Nashville for Sen. Fred Thompson, which included Tammy Wynette, Hank Williams Jr., Lorrie Morgan, and Sen. Trent Lott, nine-year-old Ashley Johnson asked for my autograph. "Why, thank you, Ashley," I said as I signed her book. "But there are a lot of people here more famous than I am."

"I know," she said.

139. Defend your wife, and don't keep it a secret.

> **That story's worth a hundred thousand votes up here. A man ought to defend his wife. Why didn't you boys bring that out sooner?**

> —*Bill Jenkins, now a congressman, upon hearing on the radio that gubernatorial candidate Winfield Dunn once had slugged a man who insulted his wife.*

140. Wave.

"I've never failed to do that since you told me about Jimmy Carter in 1980."

—Ronald Reagan, in 1984, while waving from his motorcade to a group of children. I had told him a story four years earlier about how a group of children had been disappointed when President Carter didn't wave.

141. Just don't forget that no matter how many times you've been right, sometimes you're going to be 100 percent wrong.

In 1982 I advised Don Sundquist that he could never win a congressional race. He won five times and then was elected governor. I advised Tom Beasley to give up his "long-shot idea" of privately managing state prisons and instead run for Congress. His company now has a market value of $3.1 billion.

142. Always keep in mind this advice from Minnie Pearl:

I've gotten to the point in life where I've decided that if people aren't nice, they're not so hot in my book, no matter how big they are.

143. Learn not to confuse applause with support.

I know how hard it is to clap with your fingers crossed.

—*President Ronald Reagan, responding to a standing ovation from Washington, D.C., journalists at the annual Gridiron Dinner.*

144. Remember that some things are harder than they look.

The reason most governors aren't elected president the first time they run is the same reason that most college quarterbacks don't start in their first year in the National Football League.

145. Never be too busy to meet a competent young person who wants a job.

In 1970, when I was working in the Nixon White House, a friend telephoned about a young Kentuckian who wanted a press job. After meeting her, I called Ron Ziegler, then the White House press secretary.

"I don't have time to see her," Ron said.

"You'll be sorry if you don't," I replied.

He saw her and hired her. Her name was Diane Sawyer. That interview began a media career that eventually led to ABC's *PrimeTime Live*.

146. Stay ahead of the crowd.

Michigan governor George Romney discovered one morning that civil rights leaders were marching on the state capitol in Lansing. So the governor left his capitol office, intercepted the marchers three blocks away, and marched in front of them to the steps of the capitol where he then made a vigorous civil rights speech.

147. Be proud of what you do best.

When Tennessee was recruiting the Saturn automobile plant, we hosted a number of senior General Motors officials at a dinner at the governor's residence. We served country ham, and after dinner I invited Charlie McCoy to play the harmonica. One Nashville woman came up to me afterward and said, "I'm so embarrassed. Here you have all these nice people from Detroit in Nashville for the first time and you have *that harmonica player.* Why didn't you have somebody play Chopin?"

"Mrs. Smith," I replied, "why should we offer them average Chopin when we've got the best harmonica player in the world?"

148. Keep your lines of communications direct.

A lobbyist who was also a preacher approached Lt. Gov. John Wilder of Tennessee and confided that the Lord had told him how Wilder should vote on a piece of legislation. Wilder replied, "I have a good relationship with the Lord, too, and if He wants me to vote for the bill, He should speak to me directly."

149. Don't be surprised if you and your speechwriter don't always see things eye to eye.

I once wrote speeches for Sen. Howard Baker. He told me these speeches were "brilliant"—but when he spoke he never said one word of what I had written. "What's wrong with our relationship?" I finally asked the senator.

"Lamar, our relationship is perfect," he replied. "You write what you want to write and I'll say what I want to say."

150. Don't feel obligated to accept every honor.

On a summer day in 1750, Robert Morris Sr., the manager of the port of Oxford, Maryland, rowed out to an English merchant ship to examine its cargo. It was customary for the ship to fire a cannon shot in Morris's honor. The signal for the cannon firing was to be a wave of the ship captain's white handkerchief. The sun was hot, and the sweating captain without thinking wiped his brow with the white handkerchief. The cannon salute followed immediately. The wadding of the cannon struck Morris, the honoree, who died of infection two days later.

151. When stumped for an answer, ask yourself, "What is the right thing to do?" Then do it.

My second political job was with Bryce Harlow, a wise man who had been President Eisenhower's favorite staff member. I worked for Mr. Harlow in 1969–70 while he was in charge of congressional relations in the Nixon White House. Once, Mr. Harlow told me, the Eisenhower cabinet had been in a swivet over a difficult decision. Ike went around the room. Each cabinet officer offered a different opinion.

"Unless we do it this way, it will damage national security," said the secretary of defense. "That will create grave foreign-policy implications," interrupted the secretary of state. "Because of financial implications, I must insist on a different path," said the secretary of the treasury. And on it went.

Finally, the president, becoming red-faced, said, "Well, what would be the *right* thing to do?"

The secretary of state, sitting next to the president, answered first: "Oh, well, the right thing would be such and such." And on around the table it went, with each secretary putting aside the narrow interests of his department and agreeing that *would* be the right thing to do.

"Then that is what we will do," the president said, and he sent press secretary Jim Hagerty out to tell the media.

III
Making a Difference

The best governors and presidents I have known led like Count Basie, who could sit down at a piano, tinkle a few notes, and inspire a group of musicians to play more brilliantly than they ever had before.
For these leaders, Rule No. 1 was helping others be themselves and be at their best.

Here are some other rules of leadership and of governing that I've found helpful.

152. Be skeptical, not cynical.

153. If you're going to back someone into a corner, make sure you leave them some way out that doesn't run over you.

154. Don't have a critical meeting with an important person after 5:00 P.M.

155. Let people know your core principles.

> **I'm a Republican and a Presbyterian. I fought to save the Union and I vote like I shot.**
>
> *—my great-grandfather John Alexander,*
> *when asked his politics*

156. Expect less from government and more of ourselves.

157. Make welfare as hard to get as a building permit.

158. Don't build trade walls, but tell our trading partners, "Do for us what we do for you."

159. Be as committed to military men and women as military men and women are committed to our country.

160. Remember that equal opportunity is for individuals, not groups.

161. Be proud that this is a
nation of immigrants, but
be even prouder to say,
"We are all Americans."

162. Remember that the family is the basic unit of society.

163. Remember that religion is the chief transmitter of our values.

164. Remember that those closest to the problem usually can figure out the best way to solve the problem.

> **There are a great many things that the state government should do that the federal government has no business doing.**
>
> —*Ronald Reagan*

165. Here's a good rule of thumb for deciding whether a job belongs in the government rather than in the private sector: If you can find it in the Yellow Pages, the government probably shouldn't be doing it.

166. Do whatever you can to create the best schools in the world for our children:
- Support neighborhood schools.
- End teacher tenure, and pay the best teachers a lot more.
- Give parents choices so nobody's child is made to go to a bad school.

167. Don't be surprised when the profession becomes the enemy of discovery.

I learned this the hard way when the National Education Association fought our successful effort to become the first state to pay teachers more for teaching well.

168. Read anything Diane Ravitch writes about education.

169. Read anything Daniel Boorstin writes about America.

170. Read anything Dave Barry writes.

171. Know when to stop campaigning and to start governing.

172. Remember that pioneers—not fence-sitters —helped make this a great country.

173. Spend your political capital. It doesn't keep.

174. Don't even think about not balancing your budget.

175. Think of a budget crisis as an opportunity to innovate.

176. **Don't forget that one good way to raise the average is to improve the best.**

177. Finish what you start, and don't start more than you can do well.

178. Don't be afraid to put most of your eggs in one basket—as long as you make sure it's the right basket.

179. Pick one fundamental issue and throw yourself into it with everything you've got for as long as you're in office—because sooner or later you'll wear everybody else out.

180. You might want to apply this advice about business to your class, your city, or our country:

> **The most important question is, What does the institution need most? and the most important thing to do is to get busy doing it.**

> —*Peter Drucker*

181. After you've decided what's most important and what to do about it, don't forget that the rest of your job is to persuade at least half the people that you are right.

182. Visit Monticello.

183. Visit the Grand Canyon.

184. Visit the U.S. Holocaust Museum.

185. Drive through Cades Cove in the Great Smoky Mountains.

186. Read Alex Haley's *Roots.*

187. Read Stephen Ambrose's *Undaunted Courage.*

188. Read Benjamin P. Thomas's *Abraham Lincoln.*

189. Read Judith Viorst's *Alexander and the Terrible, Horrible, No Good, Very Bad Day* to your children or grandchildren.

190. **Study to show thyself approved unto God, a workman that needeth not be ashamed, rightly dividing the word of truth.**

—*II Timothy 2:15*

Each time I was sworn into office, I put my hand on the family Bible open to this verse. It was my father's favorite.

191. Pray King Solomon's prayer for wisdom:

> **Give therefore thy servant an understanding heart to govern the people, that I may discern between good and evil.**
>
> *—I Kings 3:9*

192. Practice what you preach, but don't preach much.

193. Work a little harder than you expect those around you to work.

194. Predict less than you can deliver. Even better, don't predict.

> **Never prophesy, especially about the future.**
>
> —*Mark Twain*

195. When you're elected, don't think you're ready to host *Saturday Night Live* just because your staff laughs at your jokes.

196. And be wary of the staff member laughing loudest.

197. To stay in touch after you've been in office for awhile:
- Sit for three hours in the back of a public-school classroom.
- Take a bus to work.
- Attend a minor league baseball game.

198. If you are a governor, stick close to home. There you outrank everyone except the president of the United States. Outside of your state, almost everyone else outranks you.

199. Keep the friends you had when you were elected.

> **Never sell old friends to buy old enemies.**
>
> —*Abraham Lincoln*

200. Tell those friends that you can't do much for them until you are out of office.

201. While in office, make new friends carefully.

202. Remember that most people who are nominated by Republicans serve by the grace of Democrats. The reverse is also true. Your friends may elect you, but your job is to serve all the people.

203. For important positions, don't appoint the first person you think of. Instead, make a list of the five best people for the job without regard to whether he or she might accept. Then, begin recruiting them, starting at the top of the list.

204. Expect to be disappointed if you appoint someone to a job for reasons that don't have anything to do with whether or not he or she can do the job.

205. Write thank-you notes promptly and in longhand.

206. Exercise.

207. Smile.

208. Use your common sense.

209. Speak and write about what you really care about. You'll be surprised at how persuasive you'll be.

210. Remember that the higher an ape climbs in a tree the more his rump is exposed.

211. Schedule family time before you schedule any other time.

212. Don't underestimate the effect serving in government has on your family.

> **Many teenagers might call their family a zoo, but I think the description particularly fits my family's situation. Perhaps a more specific view would be a wildlife refuge. We are all different animals, wandering and discovering but observed constantly. We have lived in a fishbowl viewed by everyone from every angle for the past eight years. It has not been easy with my father as governor.**
>
> *—Leslee Alexander, an essay, age fourteen*

213. Don't have planning meetings that are too short.

214. Don't have operational meetings that are too long.

215. Plan together. Make decisions alone.

216. Surround yourself with people who have actually done something.

217. Place your own telephone calls.

218. Return every phone call the day it is received, or have someone call to say that you are unable to return it and why.

219. Don't even think about letting a machine answer your office phone during the day.

220. Remember that governing is a lot like playing the piano.

- **Practice.**
- **Get it right.**
- **Play nice and even.**
- **Keep it under control.**
- **Always play it just a little slower than you actually *can* play it.**

—*Miss Lennis Tedford, my piano teacher*

221. Remember that the impression people have of those who work in your office is the impression people will have of you.

222. Don't say "we" when you mean "I."

223. Don't say "I" very often.

224. Don't change principles, but learn to apply your principles to changing circumstances.

225. Find the good and praise it.

—Alex Haley

This is one of my favorite quotes. Most of the time it works better than criticism or a sermon.

226. Don't stamp it "Confidential" unless you want it published.

227. Don't expect legislators to set an agenda. That's the executive's job.

228. Don't be surprised when the smallest thing becomes the biggest thing.

229. Be bipartisan, not nonpartisan.

230. **Make big decisions in the calm.**

—Dwight David Eisenhower

231. Privatize prisons.

232. Lower taxes.

233. Spend on prevention. It costs less than trying to find a cure.

234. If you become cynical, visit a military base and have lunch with enlisted men and women.

235. If that does not work, attend a community college graduation ceremony.

236. If you are still cynical, don't run for re-election.

237. Never increase your own salary.

238. If you have to cut the overall budget, cut your part of the budget even more.

239. Don't underestimate the influence of the teachers' union.

240. Listen to the Farm Bureau.

241. Borrow good ideas and acknowledge them.

242. Don't waste time trying to make the pony express run faster or chasing after trains that have already left the station.

243. Be glad government isn't so efficient. Think of what life would be like if government actually carried out every goofy idea someone dreams up.

244. Govern the same way you shoot free throws: Practice, do your best, then put the missed opportunities out of your mind.

245. Don't even think about going to Washington, D.C., without a good lawyer.

246. Remember that when it comes from Washington, D.C., even English is not necessarily English, and math is not necessarily math.

247. **If you want a friend in Washington, D.C., buy a dog.**

—Harry S Truman

That is why, when I went to Washington, D.C., as President Bush's education secretary, we took two dogs, one cat, one frog, and our pet cactus, too.

248. Serve in Washington, D.C., long enough to get vaccinated but not infected.

249. If you stand too close to the fire, don't complain if you get singed.

250. Never let the public-address announcer introduce you at football games. You'll have enough opportunities to get booed without asking for it.

251. If you want to enjoy the game, sit in the stands, not in the president's box.

252. Take Sunday off.

253. Say "Good morning."

254. Remember birthdays.

255. Know the name of and something special about each person in your office.

256. Begin each telephone conversation with something besides business.

257. Don't write many memos. A direct conversation saves time, discourages buck passing, and encourages teamwork.

258. Do things for yourself.

> **I tell my girls that if you become dependent on others and let them do everything for you, you soon become ugly.**
>
> —*Mrs. Richard M. Nixon*

259. **Keep in mind that enough small steps in the right direction will still get you where you want to go.**

260. Don't draw lines in the sand that you can't defend.

261. Trust your first instinct, but don't act on the first piece of information you receive.

262. Avoid jargon.

263. Visit newspaper editorial boards.

264. Speak in public as if you were actually carrying on a conversation with a real person.

265. Take your turn refereeing high school basketball. It's one good way to develop the thick skin necessary for public office.

266. Try to do at least one thing better than anybody else.

267. Live at home. If we had it to do over again, we would live at home and use the governor's residence for ceremonial functions.

268. Drive your kids to school.

269. Know your neighbors.

270. Attend your class reunions.

271. Focus on what comes next instead of what went wrong.

272. Take an afternoon nap—just fifteen minutes can make a world of difference.

273. Keep your office door open.

274. Listen.

275. Follow your own advice.

276. Don't have many secrets.

277. Stay on the offensive.

278. Don't be offensive.

279. **Don't borrow trouble.**

—*Robert Louis Stevenson*

280. Keep your word.

281. Allow dumb questions.

282. Avoid dumb answers.

283. Don't be afraid of failure.

284. Remember that it is more blessed to repeal than to enact.

285. Make two-year budgets, which leaves every other year free to review, improve, and repeal programs.

286. Remember that the first job of government is to make neighborhoods safe.

287. Think of government employees as good people trying to do a good job.

288. When you are invited to testify before Congress, don't do all the talking. Remember that the main reason you're there is to give members of Congress the opportunity to appear on TV.

289. When you are in office, remember that one of your most useful powers is to convene to discuss things that are important. People will usually accept your invitation.

290. Name your proposal well. It can make a big difference. For example, the national "Right to Work" Committee guaranteed its success when it picked its name.

291. Don't talk to your children as if they were legislators.

292. Don't talk to legislators as if they were children.

293. **If you can't respect someone who holds an office, try respecting the office.**

294. Remember that no one is wrong all the time. Even a broken clock is right twice a day.

295. Don't try to know everything. Know who does.

296. If someone on behalf of the president asks you to do something for the president, ask to speak with the president.

297. Serve two terms and get out.

298. Accept gracefully the fact that you are out. Australians put it this way:

Rooster today.
Featherduster tomorrow.

299. Six reasons to move to Australia for six months when you leave office (as our family did):
1. It's warm in January.
2. It's so far away no one can find you.
3. You won't get mad about what your successor says because you'll never hear about it.
4. It's the best view of America outside America.
5. Your kids will agree to it.
6. That good Australian sunshine and humor will help you build a stronger family.

300. When out of office, expect to be confused with wide receivers, newscasters, and country music singers.

Don't worry, this happened to Minnie Pearl, too. She was on an elevator in the Opryland Hotel when a tourist said, "I'll bet a lot of people tell you you look like Minnie Pearl."

"Why, yes," Minnie said sweetly, "they do."

The tourist said, "I'll bet it makes you mad, don't it?"

301. Remember that people will remember the last thing you do.

302. **Don't be surprised when all is said and done, if more is said than done.**

—Lou Holtz

303. Don't be reluctant to ask for your predecessor's advice.

304. Be reluctant to give your successor advice.

305. Attend your successor's inauguration, but keep in mind that your role is approximately that of the corpse at the funeral: Everybody just wants to look and make sure that it's you and that you're gone.

306. Teach your children this grace that Mayor Fred Montgomery, the grandson of slaves, offered before his fish fry in Henning, Tennessee, on the Fourth of July 1994:

> **America was founded on the basis of life, liberty, and the pursuit of happiness. No matter how your ancestors arrived here, no matter what color your skin is, no matter what language your great-grandparents spoke, we are all Americans. With all of America's faults, this land is still a wonderful place to live.**

307. Cherish our country.

308. Cherish your freedom.

309. Pray for our leaders.

310. Do your part.

311. Hold on to your dreams.

Other books by Lamar Alexander:

The Tennesseans, Thomas Nelson, 1980 (with Robin Hood, Barry Parker)—People and places from a one-thousand-mile walk across a state.

Friends: Tennesseans and Japan, Kodansha, 1986 (with Robin Hood)—An international odd couple and a relationship that has flourished.

Steps Along the Way, Thomas Nelson, 1986—A governor's scrapbook.

Six Months Off, William Morrow, 1988—An American family moves to Australia to reconnect and explore the world.

The New Promise of American Life, Hudson Institute, 1994 (with Chester Finn)—Conservative essayists paint a picture of what life will be like when Americans learn to expect less from government and more of ourselves.

We Know What to Do, William Morrow, 1995—Hopes, dreams, and wisdom gathered during an 8,800-mile drive across America.